how to be afraid

Violet Graham

BookLeaf Publishing

India | USA | UK

how to be afraid © 2024 Violet Graham

All rights reserved.

No part of this publication may be reproduced, stored in a retrieval system, or transmitted, in any form or by any means, electronic, mechanical, photocopying, recording or otherwise, without the prior written permission of the presenters.

Violet Graham asserts the moral right to be identified as the author of this work.

Presentation by *BookLeaf Publishing*

Web: www.bookleafpub.com

E-mail: info@bookleafpub.com

ISBN: 9789363313217

First edition 2024

for casey

i got to love you

Not all parts

of all things

are true

But some parts

of many things

will speak

to you.

i.

the first thing i ever learned
was how to be
afraid.
be afraid, even in the safest places
because no one and nothing can be trusted
do well in school
not to make yourself proud
or because learning is amazing
but because failure
is terrifying.
you can have that haircut, if you lose 10 pounds
because being fat
is embarrassing
and embarrassment
is the worst kind of terror.
being proud of yourself
was secondary, or maybe
7th or 10th on the list because
there are so many different ways to be afraid.
anxiety.
sadness.
hurt.

failure.
terror.

panic.
always be looking out for the worst case
scenario.
count on it.
plan ahead.
don't show anyone
how you actually feel.
and never, ever reveal
how truly
afraid
you are.
because life
is being
afraid
always.
is it possible to unlearn this?
i find it doubtful,
instead
i cultivate the safety
i never had then.
i gift myself the permission
to speak up when i'm scared.
i allow myself to say no
when i feel scared into saying yes.
i find friends

who are proud of me
for getting through this day
even when i'm terrified.

(which is almost every day)
i'm learning to be a parent
to the inner me
and tell them
that it's ok to be afraid.
and tell them
this world is so much bigger
than fear.
someday, little one
you'll be surrounded by people
who will walk through fear with you
and show you the universe
on the other side.

ii.

4

ask me what it's like to live
without a childhood
and i can only answer
i don't know
what it is like to remember
cold days in september
when you were only three
i don't know how it feels to have oneself
firmly anchored in
the certainty of past events
i only know
a few scattered moments of the years
i grew from babe to child
to me
ask me what it's like to live
without remembering
and i can only answer
i don't know
what it is like to have movie-like memories that
span
more than a moment in time
i couldn't tell you what
color the classroom was or even
who was in it
besides that one photographic memory

of the chalkboard
ask me what it's like to live
without the past
and i can only answer
i don't know
what it is like to live
knowing anything but the future

iii.

there's something satisfying about
doing something secret, about
sneaking around and not telling
what you're doing, like you're
subverting the establishment in your own
pitiful way, getting what you want
even when you're not supposed to have it its like
going under the bridge not over it
taking the bike path on foot or
putting the heading on the wrong side
of the paper; it means
you're unique
you're you
you're going to do it
your way
and it doesn't matter how little you do
but it makes it easier to get by
when you know that you're
doing it different
but not exactly
not quite wrong

iv.

i keep waiting for that moment
and every time it comes, i miss it.
i wait too long, and
the moment disappears.
i hesitate,
and the opportunity is gone.
the words are on my tongue,
but i can't open my mouth wide enough
for them to fly out.
there's no way around it,
this block i have.
i just keep waiting
for the moment to come.

V.

8

my eyes
laced with tears
are closed
and my lips
with sobs
on my tongue
are closed
and my heart
crying out in pain
is walled in
and my hands
pregnant
with meaning
and words unspoken
are still
and i
myself
am closed
to you.

vi.

9

I hope that
When insects go still
They are dead,
Not suffering.
Humans can
Live a long time
Not moving

vii.

focus on the basics.
think. read. write. eat.
or don't, whichever you prefer.
its all the same to me, its not as if
i get anything out of it,
life, i mean, long and tedious,
pedestrian, now theres
another word i learned in the fifth grade
when i was first
unhappily happy
i don't even think about it
anymore, i can't stand to
admit that theres more
or that there should be,
i miss the blades and matches,
the pills that make me ill, now
when i think of them,
i miss them all, the instruments of my
slow descent into self-destruction, my
spiral
into bottomnone darkness
see, im a poet, i can make up my own
words to my own strange song, its
called poetic license, now that's a funny
concept, imagine having to get

a license to write, even the little children

who write limericks and rhymes and
think they've seen,
wrote, everything, with their own
laminated color picture card, 'poetic
license'
funny thought now, in the darkness now,
see,
i use the real word, im not that far gone,
but imagine, imagine having to take a
poetic exam,
like my history test but in rhyme,
not that i can rhyme but wouldn't that be
funny? to see
but no, the world is too silent now,
bogged
down in its own juices like pot roast
bubbling in the pan
underwater i cant say anything but
scream wetly like the dolphins
scream darkly like the orcas, they
called them killers once, too, only they
did not (or
so they say) kill themselves, slowly, like
i do, no,
they killed man, men, did they ever
I wonder

kill someone's wife or
niece or daughter did they ever
I wonder

kill someone's wife or
niece or daughter did they ever
hear a woman scream before she bled to
salty death beneath the waves
no. they are only legends, locked in
this dead house, no
beams or walls or ceilings just darkness
for floors
can you get cedar flooring the color
of darkness i wonder could you just
walk into home depot say, i want a
house the color of darkness
here, here is the flooring. and here
is the plaster and plywood and walls,
build yourself a house as dark and full
and deep as the night.

viii.

13

too angry at my own mistakes
bad choices, excuses
weakness
fear
all the things that kept me from you
all the time i wasted that will never be
reclaimed

ix.

and yet
i try
to speak
my mind
inept
unwise
to minds
unkind
and if
i lose
or gain
i find
it takes
bloodletting
to unwind
and if
i sighed
and if
i died
would someone
hear
would someone
mind
and if
i screamed

and if
i moaned
and fell
from heights
and broke
my bones
would
they know
whats in
my head
or would
i be
much better
dead
something in
my lonely brain
wants to try
to die again
something in
this mind alone
knows i am
not made of stone
something in
these tear-
filled eyes
sees a world
that i despise
sees a world

no compromise
is this such
a big surprise

16

X.

my skin
does not belong to me.
every inch they touched,
every hand i felt,
marked out an area of property,
delineated boundaries of ownership.
and now,
when my lovers run their fingers
across my face, my back, my chest,
it is not their hands i feel,
but the chill touch of those who will
always own parts of me,
ghosts that take the form of my lovers'
hands,
repeating endlessly
the touches of the past.

xi.

18

I am a blade of grass,
Bending and twisting,
Sometimes painfully,
With the wind.
Above the plains
I am a hawk,
Soaring unhindered
Through the sky.
I am the ocean.
I ebb and flow
With the tide.
I am older than the ocean,
I am ageless,
I am everywhere.

xii.

19

to watch the sun setting over the ocean
on a day of blessed peace,
to feel the breeze wrap me in warmth.
touching my arms in a gentle embrace,
to see the light fading
from a tropical sky
to find myself breathing deeply
of equatorial air
to be the open window
through which others' joyful voices stream
this is the gift that today has given
this is the living that comes before dying
this is the revelation of all that was hidden
these are the things that keep my soul flying

xiii.

20

this land is
so small
all around just bright
deep blue
perhaps it feels like home to little me
because i too
am floating in a endless sea

xiv.

21

an angel took the form of a
tiny cat to teach me a
lesson in letting go.
he came to me and whispered
in a kitten voice, "hello"
and when I knew he as
alone I knew as well I'd
have to leave
him all alone to face the
dogs and lonely nights
and still breathe
my heart is breaking not
to have him still warm
and sleeping in my arms
and I can't escape the feeling
that by leaving it is
me doing harm
but an angel came in the
form of a cat
to teach me about letting go
and it is a lesson that
I still do not wish to learn.

XV.

A very smart person once said,
Life
Is sorrow
And loss
Loss
Loss
Today I miss you.
I miss you every day.
I miss the conversations we could have had
I miss the times we could have spent
I miss your smile,
That you smiled every time the shutter clicked
Even when you were hurting.
Even when you were dying.
Your only motivation was to make sure
That we could go on without you
But let me tell you
From experience
We can't.
You said you would watch over us
But then
You left.

It's not your fault.
It's just
What is,

And what isn't.
No matter how many times I listen
To the recording of your voice
You won't come back.
It's a facsimile
Of who you used to be.
And that's where we are now
Substituting pixels and screens for real people,
real experiences
The kind you worked so hard to fill your life
with
When you understood the time bomb in your
chest
May life find me, when I'm dying
On a beautiful beach
Surrounded by friends.
You showed me the way.
But now I walk it
Alone.

xvi.

Pain
Like hot wire through bone
Like nerve fibers set ablaze
Constant, crushing, twisting
Stomach, paralyzed, makes
Each dose of medication,
Each meal
A gamble
A game
Will the pills work this time?
Will the food trip me up,
Nausea, vomiting, abdominal pain?
In between doses I lie motionless on the
couch
Moving only to change the channel
The less I move, the longer the relief
lasts
Such as it is.
The long, yawning, aching spaces
between doses.
Days upon days when I can't take the
wait
The imbalance is my own fault
My own weakness
I can't take this pain any more.

No one has any answers.
Your tests are perfectly normal, they
say.
They can't feel
Hot wires through bone
Nerve fibers ablaze
They don't live
Long nights awake when all I can think
about is this pain.
Oh, what I would give
For an empirical pain test
Evidence that we are telling the truth
Doctors that truly believe and fight for
us
Until that day I will be lying here
Motionless
Hot wires through bone

xvii.

ask me how it is to live
without a memory
and i will tell you
it's never knowing
that i was here, before,
maybe just yesterday
or maybe 3 decades ago
it's knowing my earlier self
only in pictures
(thank god there are pictures,
otherwise how would i ever
make sense of any of it)
maybe that's why i was born of
such obsessive documentarians
not even aware yet
that even their minds have been erased
and when memory comes back
it does so in the most brutal way possible
as if it wont put up with
being forgotten a second time

xviii.

27

The world tells us we all need something more
to be complete, that just one more thing will fill
the empty deep dark crack that we are feeling at
any given moment. In reality, we are all full of
cracks, and filling one just makes us aware of
another. We could spend a lifetime or perhaps an
eternity going from one crack to another, finding
something to fill them up, trying to fill up the
cracks on the outside. We would only find that
inside the darkness was even deeper, that we
were all alone, and the cracks that made us feel
broken had actually been letting in the light -
and more importantly - most important of all -
letting us connect with all of the other people
who are also reaching through their own cracks
and groping for a hand, something warm and
real and just as broken.

xiv.

everything uses this one pattern
and i can't tell if it's me, or if it's everything,
or what
seeing the pattern everywhere -
maybe - clairvoyance?
am i seeing god in everything?
everything has a universal slit code
identical to a piano octave pattern
or flute fingering pattern
i probably correlate -
oh -
second -
holy shit -
there's so much in this music
old pictures on the wall, and the albums in the
living room
i need you to know each other
and to know me
individually
so you can trust that i'm here to sweep you
away.

XV.

don't you know by now
that i can't keep a secret
haven't you heard
i'll be the first to tell
but don't worry sweetie
'bout the things that you gave me
'cause every single person here
thinks i'm high and batshit crazy

xvi.

All the wires and modems in the world
Can't bring two people close enough to touch
It's hard to have to watch from far away
Can't do anything and yet I care so much
Typed words and kindnesses can't take the place
Of human hands and doctors by your side
How can we make a difference from a distance
When life is telling you to run and hide
Just because I'm not there holding your hand
Bandaging your wounds and helping you to feel
Doesn't mean that I care any less
Doesn't make your actions much less real
Like the valiant allies in the war
I know the code and know your battle plans
But all that I can do is watch you die
And strain to reach you with my thin text hand

xvii.

No one is just one thing.
Love is everywhere, even in the depths
of darkness.
Just because you can, doesn't mean you
have to.
Old ways won't open new doors.
Everyone has something to teach, and
something to learn.
Sometimes you have to walk through
shit and vomit to get to where you really
need to be going
Not all parts of all things are true,
But some parts of many things will
speak to you.

www.ingramcontent.com/pod-product-compliance
Lightning Source LLC
LaVergne TN
LVHW021327200726
843509LV00014B/2429